MW01057342

NATHAN PETERSON

So Am I

For my family, for our friends, and for Olivia.

Maybe it's not about holding on. Maybe it's better to let go.

"We all go through these awful seasons, and in the middle of them we're thinking in days and weeks, but later we realize our best seasons of growth take years. Years is a long time to fight, and you'll eventually run out of steam, but if you can *learn to rest in the middle of the pain* - to stop fighting - to accept your current situation and *live now*, not later when things get better - that's when the most dark moments can become beautiful."

I wrote these words on January 7th 2015, the morning our fourth child, Olivia Jane Peterson, was to be born.

Heather and I had known for months that Olivia had a fatal disease called Trisomy 18 which we were told made her "incompatible with life". We were prepared to say goodbye to her that night. I've never been so scared in my life.

That night Olivia miraculously survived birth. Then her first day. Then her first week. Then months. Then her first birthday. Olivia lived 14 months - *every minute* of them - and so did we. They were the most painful and the most beautiful 14 months of our lives.

This book is a chronological recording of my thoughts and writings over the course of Olivia's life. As you read this book, you'll be re-living those 14 months with me. I hope the life and beauty which flowed from Olivia into our lives will flow into yours as you read.

The Dress

January 7 2015 (the day Olivia was born)

Heather is the most amazing person.

When we found out Olivia had a terminal condition, Heather went and quietly knit the most beautiful and extravagant baby dress I've ever seen.

A dress that took countless hours of intense focus and care and wasn't guaranteed to ever be worn.

Today Olivia wore Heather's dress and looked so beautiful.

What a natural mother and nurturer. I'm inspired and humbled by her generosity, faith, and beauty. But even more by her courage.

When fear came to her door, she chose to stare it in the face, stitch after stitch, and not turn away until something beautiful came into being. That's who Heather is.

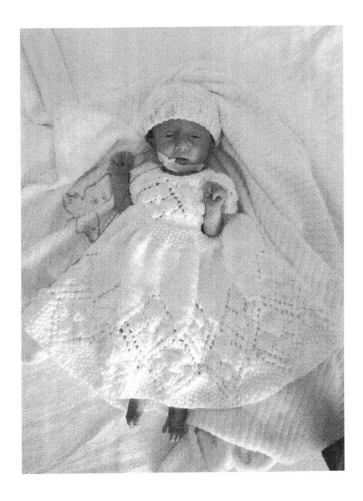

February 4 2015

Olivia is 4wks old today! We can't believe she's made it this far, but even after several close calls she's decided to stay with us for another day.

"To all who mourn in Israel, he will give a crown of beauty for ashes, a joyous blessing instead of mourning, festive praise instead of despair."

ALDI Preacher

On September 2nd 2012 I saw a tall black man with a priest collar at ALDI. When he passed me my spirit kind of jumped - like "notice this guy". A few seconds later he came back and asked, "are you born again?" "I'm sorry, what?" "Are you a Christian?" I said yes. He said "I thought so. I felt like I was supposed to come back and tell you, God's about to do great things with you." I said "Really?" He said "Yes. Be very attentive." I thanked him and he walked away.

This was one of my lowest days. I was transitioning to music full-time and feeling zero traction and like a failure. I was sure God sent him to let me know I just needed to hold on, because I was going to impact millions of people soon with my music.

I've thought about that interaction almost daily for years. Many times it's all that's kept me going.

Over the past several months, everything in our life has come to a halt. Our current season is winter. All is still. Dead or asleep. Silent. Frozen. Bare. It's a season I never want, but one I am always grateful for in retrospect. In winter, things which don't run deep are allowed to die. In winter, there's clarity where there used to be noise, and priorities are a simple thing.

Without winter we'd suffocate under the thousands of layers of identity and unneces-sary commitment and responsibility we heap upon ourselves during the rest of the year. We need winter to be clear on who we are and who we're not. Who we are in summer, when we're performing at full capacity, on stage with sound and lights - that's not necessarily us. Who we are in winter, when everything is quiet and there's nothing to hide behind and our weakness is painfully obvious to everyone - *that's* who we are.

Unfortunately, most people spend their lives avoiding winter at all costs. The highest cost is that they never get to know who they really are.

I will make music again (I have to keep saying this to myself every time I look out the window at the badly neglected band van and trailer), but that's not what the Aldi preacher was talking about when he said "great things". "Great things" isn't wowing people from the stage, or a million iTunes downloads, or letters about how my music has changed someone's life. Those are secondary results.

"Great things" is finding rest in disaster. It's your kids seeing and feeling your strength and peace and trust in a situation where anyone else would have crumbled - their core being strengthened forever, because the battle you're fighting is also for them.

"Great things" is when everything that should have created fear in you, doesn't. It's when it all falls apart and you're still ok - when you realize for the first time that fear is the enemy, not circumstance, and now you're free.

"Great things" is when we fight our inner battles instead of retreating to our addictions, and in fighting our battles, the community surrounding us is strengthened in their fight as well.

"Great things" is when fear has to give up, because the worst happened and *we are still here* - still moving toward each other and toward God and still allowing ourselves to fully trust, fully feel, fully hurt, and fully live.

March 5 2015

Happy 8wks to Olivia. Here's to 8wks of impossible joy, pain, thankfulness, fear, weakness, and victory.

March 18 2015

Olivia Is 10 Weeks Today! She wasn't supposed to live this long. She's not supposed to live much longer, but *here she is*, breathing and loving and being loved.

She's perfect and beautiful. Somehow, at the same time that she has zero to offer the world in the way of productivity and efficiency, her life holds so much meaning and everyone who meets her is changed. This is the power of a life untouched by fear and expectations. We've allowed her to just be, so she is.

I believe this same pure identity, full of meaning and beauty and inefficiency, exists in every person. We're just trying so hard to become someone, that we never take the time to discover who we already are. Eventually we give up identity and settle for occupation. While occupation can tell us about who we are, it's not who we are.

Olivia is Olivia. Her beauty comes from a lack of production. It's the reason a tree is beautiful, or an ocean, or a blue sky. It's what it is, and not what it's not.

I want to see what happens when we stop trying to be someone and start discovering who we already are. No expectations for productivity and efficiency - just being what we are, and not what we're not.

That's Who We Are

Two years ago Heather and I sat in a coffee shop and spent the entire day dreaming. I'd just stepped away from a 12yr career and the future was wide open. It was exciting and terrifying. We started the day talking about who we were, because how can you know what to do if you don't know who you are?

After some hours we decided Heather's strongest characteristics were: nurturing and artistic. Mine were: tenacious and artistic and leader. (We're a sometimes annoyingly intense couple!) We talked about what it would look like for these two people to live fully and settled on some things which have led us to what we're now doing with music.

Looking back on that day, I now understand why Olivia has been entrusted to us. Heather's nurturing has been what's kept Olivia alive this long, without a doubt. My need to do the right thing and my unwillingness to give up has helped lead us through the scariest season of our lives, as we embrace uncertainty for an indefinite amount of time. Together, we're nurturing and honoring the beauty of Olivia and her life, regardless of the cost. That's who we are.

It's so natural to decide that the best thing to do with our gifts is to use them to get what we want. But it's obvious that Heather's and my gifts have been tailored to be spent on Olivia. She is placed in the care of two people who have been specifically trained in how to care for her.

This says two things to me:

First, a strong sense of self should always lead to generosity. Many of us spend our lives trying to create and protect our identity because we haven't taken the time to learn who we already are. As long as I'm insecure about who I am and whether I'm any good, I can't be generous towards others.

Second, this isn't the God I've always pictured - always setting up chess pieces for strategic moves. This God just wants a terminal baby to have the richest possible life, for her to be adorned in beautiful garments, for her beauty to be seen and appreciated, regardless of how long or short her life is, no matter what it costs. This feels like a more accurate picture of God than my previous one, but I'm sure it won't be my last.

April 7 2015

Olivia is 3 months today. We're so grateful for our sweet little Olive. :)

I'm so scared of the future.

I'm scared my daughter will die. I'm scared I'll never amount to anything. I'm scared my kids will be embarrassed of me. I'm scared I'll get sick and not be able to take care of my family. I'm scared I'll be forgotten.

I know I'm not the only one. So many of us are scared to the point of paralyzation. Ironically, this paralyzation is exactly what brings our list of scary scenarios into being.

Fear is the real enemy, not the scenarios.

I believe the greatest battle I'm fighting, and my generation and my culture is fighting, is against fear. And fear has been crushing us. Something has to change.

We don't beat fear by working 80 hour weeks. We don't beat fear by watching 8 hours of TV per day. We don't beat fear by getting control over everything and everyone in our life. We don't beat fear by buying things. We don't beat fear by moving to a safer neighborhood. We don't beat fear by planning. We don't beat fear by winning.

These aren't ways to beat fear - they're ways to run from it, and they don't work. *You can't outrun something you're holding onto.* There's only one way to beat fear.

We beat fear by letting go of it.

Fear doesn't grip us, we grip it.

"Let go of your fear" sounds simple but feels impossible. That's because we've allowed ourselves to fear without restriction for so long. It's a drug. A habit. A vice. We have to quit, or it will continue to kill us and every generation that follows us. Fear would love nothing more, not to kill our physical body, but to distract us our entire life until we look back and realize we were too afraid to ever live. *Fear's job is to render us useless.* A resigned person is much less powerful than a dead one.

We can't afford to hold on to our fear anymore. Our community can't afford it. Our kids and their kids can't afford it.

As hard as it's going to be, this is the generation that will stop holding on to their fear. This is the generation that will sacrifice fear and develop a discipline of trust instead. A trust in God, in each other, and in our self. To be able to say at any given moment, "I am ok. I have what I need and I have what it takes. I am able to give because I don't need anything I don't already have."

Leave The Room

It's not enough to be willing to do the right thing. We have to be willing to do the *wrong* thing. To walk through the wrong door. To marry the wrong person. To take the wrong job. To spend our time and money the wrong way.

Some of us are in a holding pattern, stuck in a room we should have left a long time ago, because we're waiting for someone to tell us which door is the right door. That's not living. Living involves risk and requires trust.

It's time to leave the room.

Pick a door, trust, and see what happens.

Nothing To Add

Success is tricky. To me, it used to mean winning over the masses - national radio play, sold out shows, lots of album sales. I just don't feel like that's success anymore.

I think the reason for trying to win over the masses, in most cases, is insecurity. At least, it has been for me. Convincing millions of people that I'm good makes it easier for *me* to believe it. But it doesn't work.

For one, it's selfish and rarely results in meaningful art. But the biggest reason is this: Even if/when we convince the masses - when our album goes platinum or our book hits #1 - the voices in our head will find a way to convince us it was a fluke. We got lucky, and they'll find out we're a fraud on the next release.

No amount of external affirmation, whether from the masses or from someone we respect, will make it any easier to believe we're any good. It's a fool's errand and we end up wasting our life on it.

The truth is, *you already are who you are. There's nothing to add.* The way you succeed is by quitting the game everyone else is playing - the race to become "someone" - and instead, accepting the truth: *you're already there.*

What you're looking for doesn't come by running. It only comes by stopping, and by peeling away everything that isn't you, until you're left with *only you* and nothing else. No stage, no lights, no accomplishments to hide behind. It's the place most of us spend our lives avoiding, and it's the place every one of us longs for more than any place else. Because what if I get to that place, where everything is stripped away and all that's left is me, and it's *good*?? Success.

(And now, for the first time, you have something real to offer the masses.)

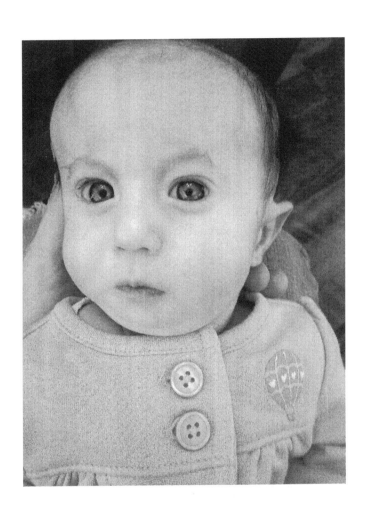

April 27 2016

I think it's 16 (?) weeks this week. Olivia's doing pretty well. She's just now coming out of a fog from a few weeks with a cold. This week the challenge is eating, for whatever reason.

We keep feeling like things are kind of back to "normal infant" status and then we start wondering, what is wrong with us? Why are we so exhausted? We realized this week that Olivia's still in the brand new infant stage in a lot of ways. It still feels like the first week back from the hospital. Not sure if it's because she's so small or it's some other reason, but that's definitely where we're at. 16 first-weeks back from the hospital. That makes me feel less guilty for being so tired!

Heather has been really amazing. Dead tired and practically disabled and depressed at times, just like me, but her capacity to still love and to even be patient with the kids has felt supernatural. I've learned about gratuitous love and beauty from Heather through this time. While most people, myself included, go into survival mode during tragedy, she has gone into nurturing mode, bringing out beauty and life wherever she can. Our nurse has said more than once that Olivia is only alive because of that love.

We are being carried by our community, still. It feels terrible, and good.

Hiding

Every morning I wake up to the same question: Will I give or will I hide?

Giving for me looks like sharing what I'm thinking and feeling through songs and writing. It looks like offering help to my wife with our family, without trying to take over. It looks like saying "no" to requests that would make me feel good but wouldn't be me. It looks like allowing time for practicing, learning, exercising. Not rushing. Not panicking.

Hiding for me looks like obsessing over the things people are thinking about me. It looks like doing work that looks good but doesn't cost me anything emotionally. It looks like pouring myself into *how* I will do things. It looks like endlessly evaluating my motives. It looks like crafting the perfect plan and getting people I respect to sign off on it.

I'm so tempted to hide. I hold onto a lot of fear. But I'd

like to say something to fear right now:

I will never quit. I will give.

I will never quit. I will give.

May 7 2015

Olivia Is 4 Months Today! What?!

Every single day for the past 4 months we've been tempted to focus on the fact that Olivia has a terminal condition, to distance and protect ourselves from the pain of losing her, to skip to the end.

Every single day for the past 4 months Olivia has breathed in and breathed out, she's loved and has been loved, giving no respect to her prognosis.

And again today, despite what we decide in our heads, Olivia is here and she is ALIVE.

We have a lot to learn about living from this little girl.

Then, Life

I don't think our situation with Olivia is as unique as it seems.

We have a little girl who is terminal. At first we were completely crippled by the news that she would probably die during birth. When she survived birth and then her first week and second week and fourth week, we were crippled by the fact that she would die any day. The extreme rays of beauty that seemingly and surprisingly emitted from her now and again temporarily distracted us from the hell we were living in, just enough to confuse us. "Wait - she's *so beautiful*. Why is she beautiful? This is supposed to be a disaster. What is this LIFE coming from her? Is she giving US life??" Just for a second, then back to the crippling fear of the knowledge we held.

After week eight we decided it was time to try to live some semblance of a regular life - we started leaving the house a bit, went on a few dates, tried to enjoy the present day since that's all we really knew we had. We're in this stage now, on week seventeen. Still mostly crippled by fear, but fighting against it and giving everything we have to live in spite of it.

We're walking through the valley of the shadow of death.

Without minimizing our situation, I think it's worth asking, how is this any different than what all of us are doing every day?

Before Olivia, I worried that my other three kids would die. I worried every time I went to play a gig that the van would crash and I'd leave my kids fatherless. I worried I wouldn't make enough money and we'd go homeless and my whole family would starve and die. Usually I coped by finding things I could control and hanging out there and dragging my feet on the things that mattered. It crippled me.

We're walking through the valley of the shadow of death.

THIS. This is what that line means. It's not for later when you're about to die. Today, every day, every one of us is walking through the valley of the shadow of death. It follows us. We all know it's there. Most of us ignore it, hide from it, avoid it, which cripples us.

We're all walking through the valley of the shadow of death.

We all know it's there.

But every now and again we're hit with a ray of beauty. "Wait, why is this beautiful? How is there life here??"

THIS. This is what Jesus taught, and *what* he was. *This* is the gospel. Not some hell-pass for later, but *a ray of beauty in the middle of the shadow of death*. "A light has shined in the darkness."

Olivia is that too. She's a ray of beauty in the darkness. She is to us the same beacon that Jesus is. Hope. Not from the fire of some afterlife hell none of us really understand, but hope for us *for today*. That *WHILE* we walk through the valley of the shadow of death, *we will not fear it*.

In not fearing it, we become like Olivia, and like Jesus - a beacon of hope - an unexpected ray of beauty in the middle of the shadow of death every one of us is walking through.

Then someone else is surprised by its beauty, just long enough to confuse fear and loosen its hold again.

Then, *life*.

Olivia is unique - there's no one like her. But I don't think our situation is unique. We're all walking through the valley of the shadow of death. We all have the same impossible choice to make if we want to really live.

"Though I walk through the valley of the shadow of death, I will not fear."

Then, life.

June 7 2015

Olivia's having a great couple of weeks. We're coming up on 5 months! We don't even know what to think anymore. So thankful. And a little exhausted.

Heather and I are still learning the same lessons as week one: how do you rest and trust and live fully and confidently when things are completely out of control?

Incidentally, I've picked up yoga during this season and the combination of that practice (holding in a difficult position with children trying to knock me down), the parallels in my voice training (singing every note from a position of complete ease and rest), and trying to be a present husband and father in our current circumstance... it's a rich and seemingly impossible lesson. One I know I'll be grateful for, later on.

Regardless of the lessons, we're most thankful for another day with our girl, little Olive.

I Will Not Be Shut Down

You keep moving. Forward.

Only you know which way is forward, but the part of you that knows, *really* knows. That tiredness and deadness you feel - it's not from the hard path, though the path is definitely hard - no, it's from the exhausting self-talk and bargaining you do endlessly with yourself.

Stop talking and start moving. Then, feel your strength emerge as resistance hits you with everything. Feel the concussions, feel the fire and the bullets, feel your arm fall off, and keep moving because *now* you know: the battle isn't the path, it's not the situation, but it's behind you, in the chair where you sat for years wondering which direction you should go.

This is living. Plenty of pain and opposition and discomfort and lost limbs - but you were never meant to make it to the finish fully in tact.

Thank God for the day we drag our nearly destroyed, totally spent, but full-of-life bodies across the finish line.

I will not be shut down.

Creating Rest

Our culture and our families are worn to threads by fear and anxiety and exhaustion from trying to control every aspect of our life. We're all on empty. We all want rest, but we're waiting for it to come to us.

We have to stop waiting for rest and start *creating* it.

Rest is more important and more scarce than ever. I don't mean sitting still. I mean *real rest*, where you're still *inside* - ok with your circumstances, ok with who others are, ok with who you are.

That's not something that comes along situationally, ever. It's something we have to create. It's a discipline. Controlling our thoughts, learning to become quiet inside, learning not to worry, learning to be present, choosing to be ok, *leading our internal dialogue*.

No one else can do this for us. They can give us toys or money or affirmation but they can never give us rest - that would be like giving someone fitness. It's up to us to put in the time, like any other exercise.

We owe it to ourselves, our family, our community, and to our culture to develop the discipline of rest - to accept rest, *real rest*, as our responsibility and not a result of favorable circumstances.

July 7 2015-
**Olivia is 6 months
old today!!**

In Debt

It's so much easier for me to overwork - to spend what I don't have of myself, going into emotional debt - than it is for me to allow time and space for personal renewal.

"There's no time for that. I'll fall behind. We'll run out of money." Etc.

American culture's addiction to spending money we don't have is part of a bigger issue, part of which is also an addiction to spending *time and energy* we don't have. There's a fear behind all of it - of falling behind.

Living this way is exhausting. We're always behind. Always in debt. Always trying to catch up. It isn't really living at all.

We're in debt. We don't need to try harder. We don't need to spend *more*. We need to do less, offer less, rest more, and build a consistent discipline of personal renewal.

If those activities make us feel guilty then it's time to change our mindset.

We have to tell ourselves the truth: Our aversion to personal renewal is not admirable - it's irresponsible. If we continue this pattern, we'll eventually have nothing of value to offer anyone.

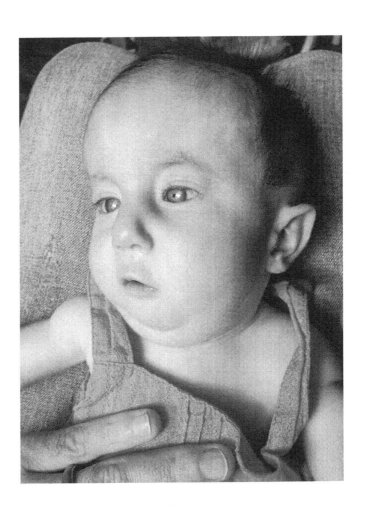

August 8 2015

Olivia is 7 months old! Still living and eating and smiling and growing. This week we met with a couple of physical therapists who are going to help us in the coming months. It's another completely unexpected step on this journey.

Heather and I are doing well. Still dead tired with periodic emotional crashing (the PTs confirmed that O is at a 1mo level developmentally, which makes sense), but we're thankful for this time and determined to *live* it, not just survive it - same as Olivia.

Responsible, Not In Possession

People keep thanking us for sharing our journey. They tell us how strong we are. I'm thankful for the encouragements and I do agree that God has made us strong for this. But I think it's easy to overlook the crowd of friends and family and even many strangers who have surrounded us.

1. We're strong some times and weak other times. But as a community surrounding Olivia and the idea she brings (that beauty is more valuable than efficiency), we are very strong. The strength people see in us is likely the strength of our community.

2. This isn't just our story. Olivia isn't just ours. I *feel* like she is, and if you try to touch her I'll probably attack you, but deep down we know she belongs to God, and her story is all of ours, and her life is for all of us.

I believe the same is true for all of our lives. I don't own my children. I don't own my self. I'm responsible, but not in possession. There's a big difference, especially when it comes to how we view sharing our lives with each other.

You Know What To Do

The question you keep asking, "what should I do?" isn't really what you're asking. You're really asking, "what will happen if I do what I know I need to do?"

You know what to do. You don't need direction. You need trust.

You don't need direction.

September 7th 2015

Olivia photo bombing Heather at a photo shoot.

Today Olivia is 8mo old!!!!

Thanks to my wife, who has poured her life into Olivia and our family for these 8 months, literally.

Our Humanity

My need to impress is immature and rooted in fear. *Letting people in*, on the other hand, is terrifying, but it's not rooted in fear; it's rooted in *trust*.

Trust - that people will get me, and if they don't, I'm still ok.

When I perform, I shouldn't be aiming for a certain response out of people. I should be aiming for a certain contribution *to* them. My contribution isn't my ability as an artist; it's my whole self, my story, my strengths and flaws, my humanity.

There aren't enough human beings walking around anymore. Plenty of teachers and leaders and superstars to like and follow and organizations to join. Plenty of people leaving this church or joining that club. But as human beings, we're alone. We're not sharing ourselves - only our product.

One of the greatest things we can offer right now is our humanity. It's scarce. The supply is low. So the cost is high. And Fear is waiting to stop us as soon as we try.

October 7 2015

Today Olivia is 9 months old! She's doing so well and we are so proud and thankful for her.

The past 9 months have been the hardest, most impossible, most beautiful months of our lives. It feels natural to look forward and wonder and hope about the next 9 months, but we choose not to. Maybe the next 9 months will be easier or maybe they'll be hell. We choose to stay in this day, the only place Olivia is and the only place we are.

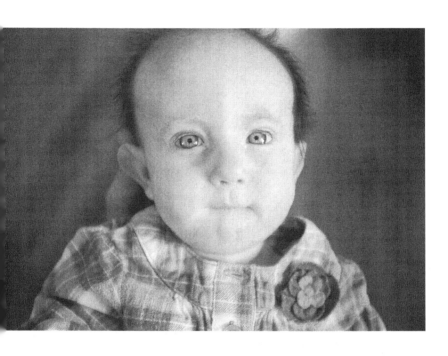

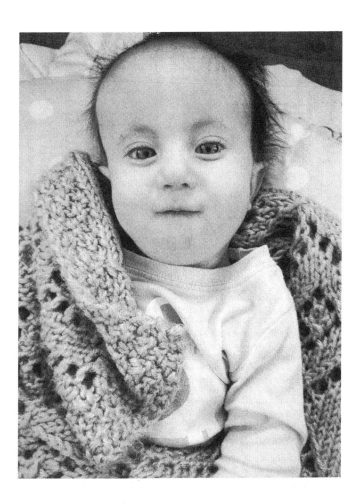

November 7 2015

Today Olivia is 10 months old! Another month which shouldn't have happened. Another month of sleeplessness and survival. Another month of living life at its most basic level - breathing, eating, loving, trying our best as parents, apologizing to our kids a lot, fighting to put effort toward our marriage, apologizing a ton, wondering why we can't be the people we picture in our heads but not letting that shut us down... another month of life.

Let whatever comes next month come - we choose to trust, to keep taking steps forward, to live life the way it is. Or try at least!

*December 7 2015-
11mo party!*

The Life Which Actually Is

My heart has been broken so many times lately. It breaks when I log onto Facebook and see friends talking about horrible things happening around the world. It breaks at things happening in our own home. It breaks at things happening in my own mind and heart.

Good.

Let our hearts be broken and stay broken. Let our expectations about the way life "was supposed to be" be shattered by the reality of the life which actually *is*.

I keep waiting for things to "go back to normal," but we can't wait for our hearts to mend before living life - it'll never happen and we'll spend our lives waiting instead of living.

Talking About
Myself

It feels weird. Writing and talking about myself and my life. I feel self-conscious and egotistical.

But really, what else is there to talk about except to share our experience of life with each other? Any other topic and I'm just pontificating. The only thing I *can* talk about with any certainty is my experience of life, *my* life. My Self.

It's not humility, as I once thought, that keeps us from talking about ourselves. It's fear - fear of telling too much or of representing ourselves poorly. Because once my image is ruined in the eyes of others, it's ruined in my own eyes. I'm not secure enough to take that risk.

So instead, we flood our culture with opinions and thoughts about things - *other* things - things we'll just change our minds about in a year. Just idle words and noise. Nothing real.

Our responsibility to each other as human beings is to *share our humanity*. Not our opinions, but our experience of life: our feelings, dreams, hopes, fears, victories, and failures. Not our theories, but our music, drawings, recipes, bright ideas, and decisions. These are real. They're the most important things to us. They *are* us. And so, *these* are the things we must share. Otherwise, the world will con-tinue to fill with the meaningless noise of a billion opinions. Nothing real.

Talking about my Self. Sharing my experience of life. It's not egotistical. It's generous. And risky. And of ultimate importance.

"Who are you to talk about yourself?" Who am I *not* to?

share our
humanity

January 7 2016 - Olivia is 1 year old today!!

Wisdom From A 36 Year Old (6 Things I'd like to tell my 35 year old self)

1. When tragedy comes, the first thing to go must be worry. It's the thing you spend the most time on which has the least benefit.

2. The inability to trust is a debilitating disease. It cuts you off from others, from God, and from your self. Learning to trust is a crucial discipline. "Trust" is better to talk about than "faith". They may be the same thing, but trust is a more concrete and helpful term in our culture.

3. Horrible things may happen, but they're never as horrible in realtime as they are when imagining them. Fear of horrible things is worse than dealing with them as they

come. Therefore, don't worry about tomorrow. This isn't just a nice thought. It's an extremely difficult mental discipline which can only be cultivated by hours and weeks and years of intentional hard work.

4. You have everything you want the most, already. The things on your wish list are only niceties. That house with the recording studio and the view, or that success you're working toward - you'd forget about them in a second if one of your kids were sick, or your wife left you, or your legs fell off, or you were starving to death. You have everything you want the most, already. So stop acting so discontent.

5. Plan less, prepare instead. If you want to be a professional, don't go to the Internet or email or your contact list. Go to the practice room. You become what you want by hard work, discipline, and consistency - not by better information and tools. The outcomes are so much farther out of your reach than you think. But preparing and disciplining yourself is completely within your jurisdiction.

6. There are no (worthwhile) shortcuts. The search for shortcuts leads to mediocrity, faulty foundations, ruined relationships, frustration, and missed life. Shortcuts are suicide - skipping life to get to the end. Your focus must be on the process - enjoying it, being content with it, remaining in it, experiencing it - and not on outcomes.

Fear Is A Choice

Our battle isn't against discomfort or uncertainty or death. It's not against any person or country or the devil. It's against Fear.

There's nothing we can do about those other things - they're a part of life. Fear doesn't have to be. It's a choice. And every time we make that choice we become more likely to make it again.

Cutting a new path is hard, but I believe our lives depend on disciplining ourselves to choose trust over fear.

AstroTurf and Fake Plants

I realized this morning during a walk, I spend too much energy trying to "get my life in order". I should realize by now, my life will never feel "in order".

Because it never ends. As soon as things are in order, something knocks it back out of order. That's just life. The only things that stay put are dead things, like astroturf and fake plants. Life is much more chaotic, and *alive* than I'm comfortable with.

There is more value in removing as many things as possible than there is in getting things in order. *Letting go*, over and over and over. Until there are so few things left that even if there's not order, there is clarity. That's really what I'm looking for anyway.

What We Choose

We have a choice. Either let hard circumstances be the lens through which we view every moment, or *enjoy* living, even in the midst of hard circumstances - accepting that there is no guarantee things will ever get "better".

We can't control circumstances, but we can control our *posture*.

This week has been very difficult with Olivia. Several all-nighters. Some big scares. We're tired and haven't been able to connect much. I feel behind with my work. But every moment we have the above choice.

Today we chose to ice skate and eat burgers with our boys. Today was fun. Today there is nothing wrong. That's not our circumstance - it's what we choose.

February 7 2015 - Happy 13 months to Olivia!

Superhuman

Two nights ago Olivia slept through the entire night (!) and the other three kids were at grandma's. That may be the first full night of sleep we've had since Olivia's been born. 400 days of sleep deprivation.

Yesterday I felt superhuman. For about an hour. Then I went to put my new powers to work, and it happened. The oh-so-familiar battle.

I may have been naive to think all I needed was sleep, and then I'd be "back on track". I'd be productive and efficient and strong and sharp. I'd be a good friend again. I'd write a full album in one day. I'd finish all the unfinished things. All the things my "true self" longs to do, if it just had some sleep. I should have realized, giving strength back to my true self would also mean a revitalized false self.

I felt superhuman for about an hour. The rest of the day I felt more like a crazy person. I felt twitchy. My mind was in 40 places at once. I couldn't focus on anything. Every good idea was met with two or three reasons why it would never work. Schizophrenic. I might as well have not gotten any sleep! So frustrating.

Then, last night we had one of the worst nights of sleep ever. I may have slept an hour. Around 5am this morning, still awake, patting Olivia's back, I felt angry at her. I know that's terrible. It's obviously not her fault. But I was just so close… to something. To a normal life. To a productive life. To a life where I make plans and then carry them out. Where I'm a productive and successful human being. A strong man.

Of course, this is all completely contrary to everything I've been learning and writing and saying at my shows for the past year. But just because you know something doesn't mean you understand it, or believe it.

Around 5:20 Olivia fell asleep, and I couldn't.

It's not her fault. It's not anyone's fault. It's not even my fault. **It just is**. That's a mature thought: It just is. This is life and I accept it. It's not something to be changed or manipulated. It manipulates us. All we can do is let go and surrender to the current, trusting its ability to take us where we need to go.

"In repentance and rest is your salvation. In quiet and trust is your strength."

Our *strength* lies in our ability to *let go*.

Not in our ability to accomplish. Not in our ability to impress. Not in our ability to look good. Not in our ability to acquire. Not in our ability to win.

This is true when we're walking zombies, when we're sick on our back, when we're grieving. It's also true when we're at the top of the world and all approval and all resources are ours.

Our strength lies in our ability to trust, not to control. To rest. To be quiet and do nothing. To be still and not step in. Even when there are tornados all around us.

Yesterday was a good reminder: Whenever (if ever) we get our strength back, our sleep back, our band back, our time back… our posture of quiet, rest, and trust must remain the same.

In Our Suffering

I'm overwhelmed by the pain and uncertainty so many of our friends are going through, not to mention our own.

The picture I've had for my own life for years has been of walking into a dark room. There's no telling what's there, how big the room is, or where it will lead. Just darkness.

As bad as I want to know the answer to "where will this lead?", I think the dark room was never meant to lead to some other end, but is the end itself.

The dark room is life. Full of uncertainty, unexpected turns, and unlimited chances to fear… or to trust.

This is living. To not be afraid. To trust. To rest. To embrace uncertainty and not run from it. To live fully and gracefully, even in the midst of darkness and death.

"When darkness falls and I can't see, when I am blind, your hand is over me… When the road is long, when all hope is gone, in our suffering we will rest in You."

March 7 2016 -
14 Months

Hit Record and Sing

Yesterday was a typical yet maybe slightly more dysfunctional than usual day. I knew I wanted to record the song "Rest In You". Once family things were squared away I went into the studio. Here's what happened:

1. As soon as I was in the studio I felt a strong urge to re-evaluate the microphone I was about to capture my vocal takes with. "What if it's not the right mic? My work will be diminished." So I hit up the internet to find my answers which we all know is a very straight-forward place to find answers. 1.5hrs later I was no closer to answers than when I started. I now had a list of 25 mics I needed to try. Worse, I felt self-hatred rising. "WHAT am I doing?!" At this point in our life, time for me to get work done is very rare. There are entire days and sometimes weeks I can't work. When I do get that time, it's precious.

2. Now I've got very little time to do my important work. I was literally pacing around my studio, furious with myself

for not just recording the vocal track. I was so angry. "I'll NEVER get anything done." "I'm broken." For a moment I pictured smashing all the gear in my studio. I was on the edge of rage.

3. I dragged myself from my enraged pacing to the center of the studio and started singing warm-ups. That's the first step. 15 minutes later I was warmed up. I dragged myself from the middle of the room to my laptop, pulled up the session, and hit record. Two seconds later my 3yr old daughter, Ruth, started banging on my door. More rage. "Why is this happening?" "Why isn't Heather taking care of Ruth?"

4. I dragged Ruth upstairs, feeling all of the anger I'd felt toward my self now directed at her and Heather. I dropped her on the floor, gave Heather an angry look, and went back down. "Great, how am I supposed to sing when I'm angry?" Two seconds later, Ruth is back. I repeated my angry return of Ruth to Heather. Back down to the studio. Hit record. Ruth is back.

5. I quit. I went upstairs and put my sweats on to go for a run. I'll never record this stupid song. Then Heather grabbed Ruth and I realized I could go running, or possibly still record. I went down to the studio and hit record again and started singing. (BTW, that's the first time I've recorded in sweats. I have no idea why, it's not like you can hear them. This opens a lot of possibilities.) I completed 5 pretty good takes and then realized the record button

wasn't hit. !!

6. I chose to regroup, hit record for real this time, and did another 5 takes. By take 12, my voice was tired and I knew I needed to stop. In the past I would have pushed to take 25 and hated myself, but I've learned the hard way that you can push through a lot of things, but not singing. Time to stop. I was depressed. I wasn't happy with anything I'd recorded.

7. I sat down and researched mics for another hour. Frustrated with the day and with myself.

8. I decided, just for education's sake, to do a rough mix of the final take and listen back. It actually sounded pretty good. This is the part where everything shifted.

Something hit me, which my mind was ignoring all day: *THERE IS NO DEADLINE. I'M NOT BEHIND.*

"Time is not running out. There is not someone chasing you down. You are not going to drown."

Where was this anxiety and feeling of being behind coming from? I think it's the same place it's come from for the last 20 years of my life. My self. For some reason I've always told myself that I'm behind. I need to hurry. I need to catch up.

There's a phrase I've run across in voice training. "Don't let your breath get ahead of your voice." Without going into much detail, picture the voice as a 2-part instrument. You have the breath which is the source of energy, and you have the vocal folds which are the source of resistance which creates vibration, which we call "voice". Generally, most voice problems are caused by an imbalance between these two parts. Letting the breath "get ahead of the voice" means we're pushing out more breath than the vocal folds are resisting, which results in a "breathy" voice, which leads to irritation and fatigue and a weak voice. An inefficient use of energy. That's why singing "harder" doesn't always make you louder.

For some reason I've always told myself that I'm behind. To compensate, I've always been in a hurry. I need to do more, fast. I need to release this song ASAP. It's not about money. It's certainly not about art. It's about catching up. As a result, I create an imbalance of energy. I'm pushing with more effort than the reality of life calls for. The reality of life says I can release a song every quarter or *year* if I want. No one will complain. My inter-nal voice says I need to release a song every month. So I push hard. This leads to fatigue and a weak "voice" (in life, because no one can say what they need to say when they're constantly feeling pressure to say something profoundly useful). An inefficient use of energy, and of my life.

9. The day was over. I closed my laptop, went upstairs, and watched a movie with my family. I felt happy. Even though the recording I did that day may not have been

a "keeper", and even though it took me the entire day to hit record, *I did hit record.* And so today, even if by only a hair, I won against Fear. I made progress. Not just with my project, but with my battle against Fear and anxiety and against lies.

Tomorrow is another day and the battle will continue. But I'll remember what happened yesterday. So will my enemy. Time is not running out. This battle isn't about today or this week or this year. It's a lifelong battle, and even a tiny step in the right direction, repeated over and over throughout life - if we keep crawling forward and dragging ourselves an inch at a time toward the finish - will eventually lead to victory. My victory today was not about recording a perfect take. It was about not giving up. The enemy isn't trying to mess up our day. He's trying to kill us - to stop us completely. When he realizes, and when WE realize, that we will never quit, no matter what, the battle shifts. I believe we've been given this power. It's what we'll celebrate this Easter. The same power that raises the dead, the same power that sustains Olivia, is the power that enables us to take another step forward.

Today, most of us will probably screw up 99% of it. It's ok. That's not the important part. We know what our other 1%, our "record button" is. It could be picking up the phone. It could be taking one of our children aside and having a conversation. Or touching our spouse on the hand and looking them in the eye and saying what we need to say. It could be giving a gift. A kind word. Quitting a job. I don't know. But you do. **In the midst of your self-hatred and enraged pacing and incessant avoidance, drag yourself out of it and hit record and sing.** Yes, most of the day feels wasted. But we will not let that determine what happens next.

This was the last recording I made while Olivia was still alive. I decided to keep the track as the final take. I will love this recording forever.

March 11 2016, 2:30AM

Olivia's sick again. :(She's very congested and throws up when we feed her due to gagging on all of the phlegm. We're back to syringe feeding and oxygen. Trying to get her to fall asleep now...

Last night Olivia took her last breath.

She was in Heather's arms, against her momma's skin - her favorite place.

I'm not sure what else to write. I don't feel like being inspiring right now. But I am so aware of the thousands of you who have prayed for Olivia daily and I didn't want you to go through today not knowing. She was yours too.

We feel a lot of things right now. But for now I want to express our thankfulness...

Thank you, all of you, friends and family and complete strangers from all over the world who carried us as we carried Olivia. We wouldn't have made it through the first night without you, rushing into our hospital room and holding our heads and praying things we weren't able to pray ourselves. We wouldn't have made it through the first week without you, washing our floors, bringing us food, sitting through the night holding Olivia while we tried to sleep. And you continued to pray and help and cry and hope with us, and for us. You carried us while we carried her. Carrying Olivia was a group effort. THANK YOU for helping us do this. Thank you on behalf of me and Heather, our kids, and especially Olivia.

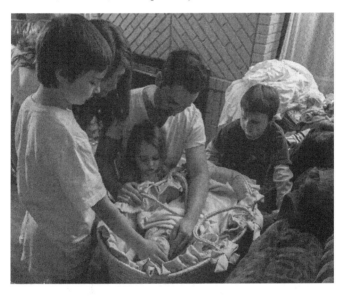

Thank you, Heather. You did SO. GOOD. Well done, faithful servant, faithful wife, faithful mother. Everyone had a part, but it was your hands and your body which directly gave life to Olivia every day of her life. She lived through you. You nursed her non-stop day and night. You carried her every day for 1 year, 2 months, and 4 days. And we all know you would have done it for twenty more years if you had the chance. You are a warrior. You did it. I'm so proud of you. Thank you for being my daughter's mother.

Thank you, Jesus. For choosing us to be the ones to carry Olivia. For preparing us for years to do it. For providing EVERYTHING we needed to do the job. For giving us supernatural strength on a daily basis. For surrounding us with people to help us. For being with us every moment. We know you love us. We know you love Olivia.

Thank you, Olivia. I love you. You taught me about beauty, life, and strength. I am honored to be your dad. And I know I'll see you again. I can't wait. I miss you.

Eulogy for Olivia

I can't believe I'm writing words for my daughter's funeral. How do I reduce what just happened into words? How do I reduce Olivia into words?

When Heather was pregnant with Olivia and we received the news, that she had a disease and wouldn't survive more than a few hours, I distanced myself from Olivia. It was subconscious. At one point I realized I hadn't talked to Heather's belly the way I did with our other kids. I never felt for kicks. I avoided naming her. I remember realizing that Fear had stopped me from loving my daughter. Maybe she wouldn't survive her first day, but she was alive today. *Living*, for me, looked like giving her a name, and talking to her. It looked like giving her my love. Becoming attached, knowing one day soon I would have to say goodbye. Fear said to stop. But Life said to be her daddy. I chose to live.

Meanwhile Heather knit a dress that took months to finish. It was beautiful. It was probably never going to be worn. I could hardly understand the amount of love and COURAGE it would take for her to make it. Olivia wore that dress her first day. She's wearing it today. Fear said not to make the dress. But Life said to be her mommy. Heather chose to live.

Heather's choice to make that dress pales in comparison to the decisions she made from that point on and continues to make even this week. The dress is a picture of the love and nurture that Heather wrapped Olivia in every single hour of her life. Over 10,000 hours of continual decisions to live, when Fear said to stop.

We Petersons don't quit very easily. We don't listen to authority the way we probably should. I think God knew that when He chose us to carry Olivia.

Olivia wasn't *supposed* to make it through her first day. She wasn't supposed to make it through her first week, or month, or see her first birthday. She wasn't supposed to be able to nurse, or smile, or dance, or laugh, or drink from a cup. She had a sense of humor! If I made a fart sound she would smile and then make her own. She wasn't supposed to do much of anything. And she *couldn't* do many things. Still, her beauty and life reached across continents and changed the way thousands of us look at life and the world and God. She couldn't hold her head up, but that was ok - we could do that for her. She couldn't eat right or breath right, but that was ok - we could do that for her.

And while we carried her, she impacted thousands upon thousands of people and generations to come with her life and with her beauty.

Similar to Olivia, we felt completely disabled most of this year. We couldn't hold our heads up. We couldn't wash our floors or do our laundry or shovel our driveway; many times we couldn't find the strength to pray, but that was ok - our community did it for us. While we carried Olivia, they carried us. The entire 14 months, we have been carried. And when our friends weren't there and we weren't able to be there for each other, we rested on God's repeated promise, that He would be there no matter what. And He was. We're so thankful to our community and to God - thank you for carrying us.

Olivia was and is our beautiful daughter. We miss her more than we can put into words. The pain is almost unbearable. But we wouldn't give up one minute of this pain or any of the pain or discomfort or inconvenience or insanity or terror of the past 14 months, for anything in the world. Because this. is. life. And not only do we accept it; we embrace it.

I can't reduce Olivia into words, and I refuse to try. I won't be reducing her into songs either. But I will attempt to honor her and reflect her beauty in the way I live my life. I don't think we have a choice. Olivia is a part of us now. Heather and I and our kids and family and many others will never be the same. So we honor Olivia by choosing to *live*, today, whatever that looks like. Fear will say to stop. But in the pain, the discomfort, the terror, the not-knowing, we will choose to live.

Thank you Olivia for teaching me about life. Thank you for letting me gaze upon your beauty for so many sleepless nights. Thank you for living for so many more days and months than you were supposed to - like a little warrior, you fought to live the life you were meant to live, every day of it. You did it! I'm so proud of you. Thank you for letting us carry you. We love you, and we will see you and hold you again, Olivia.

Live, today.

Maybe it's not about holding on. Maybe it's better to let go.

We all go through these awful seasons, and in the middle of them we're thinking in days and weeks, but later we realize our best seasons of growth take years. Years is a long time to fight, and you'll eventually run out of steam, but if you can *learn to rest in the middle of the pain* - to stop fighting - to accept your current situation and *live now*, not later when things get better - that's when the most dark moments can become beautiful.

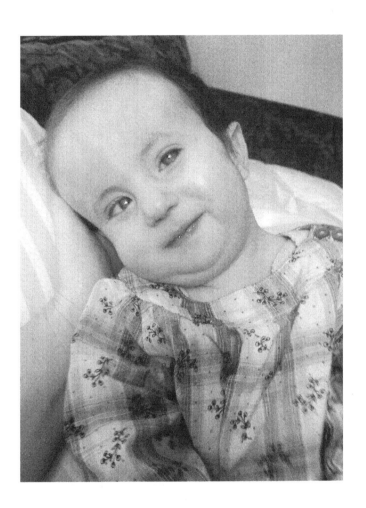

Nathan Peterson is a singer/songwriter from Illinois. He and his wife Heather are the parents of four children, Jude, Charlie, Ruth, and Olivia.

More about Nathan here:
nathanpeterson.tumblr.com
helloindustry.com

56839585R00063

Made in the USA
Lexington, KY
01 November 2016